A Mammal of Style

A Mammal of Style

Ted Greenwald

& Kit Robinson

ROOF BOOKS
NEW YORK

Cover & interior design by Kyle Schlesinger
Cover photograph by Ahni Robinson

Thanks to the editors of the following publications in which parts of this book first appeared: *Shiny 14* (Michael Friedman) "Fuse Hat Nito"; *onedit 12* (Tim Atkins) "Returns Native"; *Antennae 11* (Jesse Seldess) "Street Furniture"

 This book is made possible, in part, by the New York State Council on the Arts with the support of Governor Andrew Cuomo and the New York State Legislature.

Roof Books are distributed by
Small Press Distribution
1341 Seventh Street
Berkeley, CA. 94710-1403
Phone orders: 800-869-7553
www.spdbooks.org

Roof Books are published by
Segue Foundation
300 Bowery
New York, NY 10012
seguefoundation.com

CONTENTS

FUSE HAT NITO

ION THIEF ACE

You get your head around it
A secret location, unfolded
Head east
Roll by studying friends
Manufacturing rhythm
One of those games, just about
Tomorrow if that
They're good people Good people
Run out of difference
World outta here
Kiss the ground walking
Round the door
As they one-remove the chains
People like that

SPAN JEAN PROB

We have a cannibal
You picture a boat
Usually in bed, dreaming
The image can fly
Crows' feet stalking the eye
Creates spacewear
Seem to vanish Seem to vein
Beautiful Mexican distress *savoir*
All call for Philip's drive-by
See you soon See you some
Drugs on edge Bring the letters
It's a big foot continent
Play with one familiar face
Enter: Trombone

TRICKLE COMP

In 1934
Almost news level
Needless boil theme
(Lowlying aria)
Plays the card *didn wanna*
Always dine being hidden
And race across
Doing it (the traces) in Chinese
Clearly doing it the traces
A recent workshop saying
Not knowing it
About how relevant here as to worry
Ping pong already Balzac
Last work together on the ness

LIFT HOOD

As the meeting continues into the wee-wee
The freak stays in the picture
Nights under the stove pipe
Wireless piano shoes
Vast armies in *negligées*
Go with it!
Talking the, all the time, talk
I green red yellow
Edge elbow into arrowhead city
Which colors!
Coffee noble femme
The Bomb's the least of worries, ours
Show and tell the quinine
You got your head somewhere

LATH TALK

Charges were dropped
Just doesn't add up
Rock 'n' roll warehouse is opening It's windows
You must be nuts It's curtains
Skinflint armchair, bone-dry riverbed
Cede the air
Similar to being another planet
Whatever you're *howdy* into paraphernalia
The heart goes *wump* intercept
No deeds, facts, too many, need less
The space between you and *mi mi mi*
Freezing your legs *so so so*
Ongoing semi-overwhelming susceptibles
Kissing your ass

MOUND CO

Everything will be *fa fa* fine
Midway through now, the cantilever section
Count as friend Counter below a picture
Industrious humming united *re re re* states
People we listing to music
It might not even be that *waa*
Would have wanted us to do
What's that tell you
Make what it calls it
Picks you up Repeats you
Far and away For and again
Comes back around to meet us
Foreshadowing things commando bespoke
Manufacturing with me

ODES OF DIFF

That's why it takes all these years
This mean it goes without?
What's the difference?
Sayings, what's on your mind
Can do, who can do the average
Dig in memory all a way snake
Stand by to remain
But what he's done to deserve *is*
Crisis node now
A fair catch calls for a good catch
The sun bores my whole head
Bring on the friends just because
Stand and declare the difference
More power nice nice

POLES CLAW

Got off getting on a train
Going we R to reflex city
Not going on
The phone's off the hook
Not gonna do no more
Not only did it squirt through the legs
Dew on grass about to snap
Tomorrow if necessary
Begins to shed snap-on tools
Mash my potatoes
Drive out the kitchen
Big fat in the tatts
Water powwows over new car
I can relate

LIGHT ATCH

Understand run-up involves element uncertainty
Evenings do a man in
Five beats in a tugboat cell
Revolutionary arbitrary GOP (or *gop*)
Try listening, can't get
A guiding light
Station to stream
A lever to personal gain
That's perfect Thanx munch
It's not like It's a pitchers' duel
Glad hand to see-saw what you think
Can't play those tix
Long time no mention
No ticket no cry

TOY SART

Taken for a right
Okay, nice pix, talk tonight
When you let it ride
So-so see you, quoted in a history of today
Another grapefruit day
Run out of difference e're last night
Twilight baffled investigators
Hope all's well with you in
The Americano raises
Another phone call Another raises
Fold in a crowd
Your eggs, how you like 'em, now?
Adult audience neglects a duple bind
Who wants to *no-no?*

CHANT VING

People like that, you know M
Playball wishful thinking
The mind *is* the store
Going out to dinner in a movie
Universes stream in parallel Ls
Watch something at home
It could be different
Subjunctive it a funny way to show
Swing factor levels and dials K
Night, don't fall like sleeping I
All ye who enter
She sleeps into he rumors
Words of the door, man
Do you live here, live

YON SHIITAKE

I'm a strange myself
Totally personality left off go-go gaga
Please accept the N closure
Shining moment mumbling *something something*
Taken from the other me
If you think think it about it
Normal speed matches quick cuts
In a stand-off with jag
You were, like, under stood it all, you all
Our lady of quad loop
Weekday theater edits in the eye
Kick rebar, man dingbat
The candleholder poureth over
Open 24/7

DOWN OWN

In the English manner
Is there a lesson, any, in North America
Classic lines regular meter
Never mind them, don't I never
But then again, again, I don't ever
It's a dream Dream of interpretation
Dinner in, poetry out
Two-tone towns ago
Like (*like*) a picture tube
Been asking for
What you forget
Ask the night before
The way a watch is set *oh, night before*
A variety of other mohairs

GOV NASDAQ

And the time may come, if we are wise
Hone lizard bricks
Rushing rushing rushing
Beat replacement appetite
Pleasure and profit in another *the other*
The singer now the sun
Make way up the Atlantic snot
Switch from down to up
Better get out, don't look good
Watch five different yam games
So wanted better for it, you
The elevator's out of surface
A variety of otherwise motels
Make your own omelet *om*

RETURNS NATIVE

Good morning Pay attention It's experiment subject
What think you Don't let anyone con you
Beware of monotheist I copy you What nice nice
The road to Palace Theater is paved exits
Cloudy word eventualities None of above's weather

Blue U-turn skies International language: Piss off
River towns take drubbing Nothing to U write
Home who-ever-sees Donate your ear
20 men scramble from a be would crave One or other othern
Takes looking at (whether)

City fog open sleep broken Got out before bubble
Vote big fucken deal For business to fill pipe
Click dreams shake habit long day early Concern about voice done
Thy will be doneth bad things Stock up on later opinion
Talk time way up in stretch Careful not book overdue

Two hands still spending Night black lit sighs in afterthought
Return trip boom back done nearly As we'll shortly
One third eye season All in day's berth
Valentine coming
And out is going

Is that good a number? Wanting say don't
Say river roadie Will cubes play?
No word from treasure hunt An agenda's suit
Pieces of eight ass No benchmark no gigabit pipe
This train don't carry Lay at idol heart

A secret legible message These days go fast wake up wide
Scrap portrait stack cash car gone In plain sighting hide
Spoken quorum buzzes sensing Simultaneous concentric
Fan of days Widow of opportunity
Defenistry regime changeling Crank sleep back onto pan

What you get is what, what say? Every given nigh, away
Acceptable in sex lane Incremental wampum on rack riddle
Destination flapdoodle hokum In tact with virus highway
Good old human dailies Lemme know when you get, if get
Excuse: post pardon depress

Pay more costs own Drink out of cart before fire horse
Drive grand piano through key Diagram acceptance
Absorb in reading coasters Run don't walk Blue Mule
Go long get longing
D fence makes good

Of deep snow soma no word Now what
Sleeved selves one no Place name here whereabouts
A bird in snow is work too if Know how
First step to forget
Small in statue

Never-before-seen edit Rain in valley
Turning snow at night Footsie footage
No one knows new Pale sky head over
Cloud bank between Come away away thinking
Whatever want: mean Turning who knows what

Stay at low bandwidth Up word and down
Look both castaways Don't knock time, space
This parking lot is huge Fishing before Xing
Task someone 2 take
Doc U meant dear

Sketch shadow out Some numbers bump others what?
Jostle memory sticks thumb drives Hand with hers paper rink
Lotsa lotto stuff Rolled into one, which?
Math is radio silent Picky five anythings
Fabulous doors premier

Tales from creep The autumn passed, like
The fall (you fell) Squishy territory
Important searches Spring passed, like
A step (you stop) After 400 days
Any and head all-purpose

Clouds of undoing (necessairily) Publish your photo in paper
Surprise It's almost
Like as not, dress negative Publish your photo in paper
Baby Baby Tongue lens towels vowel
The catlike's still damp Publish your photo in paper

Language will see you now Lines disavowal
Tree's in forest fallen A lot of thinks to do
This my nearly native Returns exchange
Last thing should Nice talking you
Not flat

Maybe deep downish Standalone ad one-off hoc
Could not thinking stop The product millions of noises
Smoking's all about Puts us squarely
The best ways respond Eyeball to eyeball
Is people so inspiring You can put money on

Who said shoe said Back in garage day
Unless putter the dotter Total world fine-ass
Bring extra picture Gateways showing up
If nothing Elsie The theory of design experience
Eyes of the sea of doors Mind as minders

Stood for about an houri Keep it real, sire
Sands pile up on brain-quick With a walk of side
In roadside shoulder stand Voice dislocates figure
Secondary time Sorta with kinda
Even in day, time stand for Drains into auspices

The real reasons for are the war The car sits outside door
Is only ballet good for You don't know the answer but then you do
We are in all *Mon ami* first causeways
Brooklyn and the Bridgettes People familiar look
Music circulates lag Tears going down on checks

Peoples of that elk Baby rode a here plane
The head likes brew-ins How dojo what's doing
Flares and chaff Heart goes with the zags
Arriving spring air Serial killer music
Lawn in part, C lover Next-gen joy juice

The world will be same More than somewhat
Lower right hand Only different History touches
Here is receipt A kind once so happy
Check a line for For all of Enter later
In book of light Using a ruler so longer last

Best friend tells (on) Wonderful world of
Interest, self Count (on) not if but whence
Tells on you, time will Combines to produce of thee
Nations, united Want a lot form
Missile fascicles byway Air lines up vote

Just say backwards into Look for sighs of
Shoulda be doing The rhythm of story easy
Go forward and multiplex What!
Stops Intervals farm a bed lake
For perpetual pre-game Is as if a

See saw in half a tip-off Band of bothers
Manually freeboot Important to static
Off wheels, curbs with Operates on different planets
Listen to mi Differential Black car black helicopter
Paradise street furniture Fastened to soundlings

Overcast momentary eclipse Machinery of fiction macro
Kill me in hair Duly notational
Arrives all spazzed out Becoming subtlety about
Almost watermelony a little In nation's capital
Need less in haystack

Call about cartoons Storm blows cherry blossom mind
Gut jaunts coast to coast trip round Was young (was you?)
Relationship sutures Inside 36 hours
The territory is no message Desert tympanum inserts
Fear not exactly, no, not fear

Thunder claps hands down Taken in by talking all
A more terrible sometimie Notional spokes of road
One thin novel dime A same time sleight
So was I The road bears witness
(Or something like)

You like it like this In Capitol shoes the heels
Onslaught blurred of photography Was I was so
A place of bad hair Melting away many of buildings
Wash face and hands Unavoidable in factoid
If were you I were

Anarchical whiteboard mass As we now know
Hand-to-mouth outer There are only eyes in all
To be look out of Left wondering, right for a good
Bunch of thing hinges
Equally frankly

STREET FURNITURE

FIRE HOUSE AND CROWDED THEATER

When all is said virtually
Voice drops do whisper
Well-wishers with access
To home range audience
One bare witness
So difficult to believe

Fantasy is ability to believe
Better to really live than virtually
Otherwise assumes cloak-and-silent witness
At other end, stage whisper
Inaudible to audience
Enjoys front-row backstage access

Do you have access
Card? You better believe
It the audience
Is virtually
Everywhere, you whisper
With no one to witness

The no-nonsense witness
Without access
To the whisper
Number, believe
You me because virtually
Anything possible audience

Ladies and gentlemen, wonderful audience
Can I get witness?
With all due respect, virtually
Got wheelchair access
Cracked up to believe
Still banana trees silently whisper

Don't speak above a whisper
Because from an audience
Appreciation perspective I have to believe
We're safer here than in a witness
Protection program picking up trash on the access
Road to where you might as well crash virtually

Virtually anyone can whisper
Secret access code to audience
One witness dying to believe

NO STANDING

The rings they're in exchange
Please, try the rational
Even if you be somebody
The code, she make you zip
Despite what you have
Hinging you a long, a string

Pull the string
It's your voice in exchange
Many metals, this you have
Organize a donor organ rational
Place in the by rights spot, zip
You're a *big man Somebody!*

They call you Somebody
Putting words on a string
Big finish dip with zip
Look up, at this rate, current exchange
Job one, step river, algorithm rational
Need you gotta a lotta have

Could be you don't have
The makings of a somebody
Plan to make appearance rational
Theory along which you string
Pretend looks, an exchange
Enterprise systems throughput zip

Top down manage horizon zip
Something *it* the eyes have
But only after, in exchange
Not everybody is somebody
Body parts on a string
As for a weather which is rational

But, but, remove e from rational
The e gives vowels their zip
Clear nouns bring string
Tie up with thoughts you have
No, no, not just *Somebody!*
It's time to make exchange

First exchange the rational
Your Somebody e returns to zip
Have the cloud house lower string

ON THE OF OF LIVING

When you think about it
What you know now, knew then
Be too much for one brain
Hence importance of third term: when
Let us represent moment as digit
Such as zero one or n

Yes and no represent as y & n
And before you know it
Fork in road looks like just other digit
Like water under bridge only that was then
I'd like to go, er, can't say when
Says man in seersucker brain

Leaf of grass grows out of brain
Trolley stop J-K-L-M-N
Don't ask me why, who, what, where, when
People looking for it but this is it
And then, he tied her to railroad tracks... and then?
Uh-uh. And then along came Joe Digit

Something there is that does not like a digit
Anybody with half a brain
If you are on the bus then
You seem like nice message in bottle n
Tear drops tear at architecture of it
When ready to get off just say when

Handy man rears ugly head when
In the course of humid events no digit
No fly zone now you see it
Gauls love big think brain
Riding on the L&N
But what you think you gonna do then?

You say am here whole hog, if so then
Get real, do not pass go, wonder when
To build in room for any number (n)
Plus one equals stand-up digit
Sitting in on an alp on the brain
Which is fine, as you feel it

Just now it occurs to then
There's no brain there just hair where
This solitary digit aspires to an upside-down n

YELLOW BROKEN LINE

I have delivery
Bring your best angle
You have it take
You some know business
Complete panda moan sensation
We first meet Plato in his cave

The Greek Philosophers they love Plato's cave
They believe delivery
Shipping and handling is today's sensation
See from POV angle
In sigma, mind own, your business
Move deeply take from take

Western Civ only the lonely one take
We bring out in us the cave
Novice masters attend a business
Listening for a certified especial delivery
The light plays its own angle
Within park is golden sensation

At first, a mere sensation
Something leave or take
Winter from snow's angle
Cloud of unsnowing in a cave
Angels prepare putti to delivery
Without any naught real business

Nobody's business
Blip sensation
Cake makes way for cake delivery
Angels are on the take
Adorable, ready to cave
Obtuse isosceles, but a cute angle

But not just any angle
It's the taken angle of business
Anglish Philosophers squish with their cave
All-over overall sensation
Tape masks each take
Bell-like or rotundra delivery

Delivery remake recuts angle
The take hiss means business
Plato's sensation makes cave

SESTINA TURNER

If you go down wait a second
To the river get your heels warm
People on river remember previous
Outing you were new on scene
Did not yet have big yellow brain
Didn't recognize user error no lie

But now you think you get to lie
With riverboat queen well on second
Thought maybe you better scrub said rubber brain
Before you go off half klooked warm
Your hands at fire at scene
Of crime not original but previous

This is why you cannot rely on previous
Slides because everybody knows statistics lie
Are you ready to be rescued? Scene
Three act tooth talk to you a second
Ago musta been mistaken have warm
Fond wish summer hammock habit brain

What we have here is a brain
Size problem said Ike the Previous
Would you like your calves cool or warm?
Two feet looking out the window lie
High above panoramic Jack Flash the Second
Time is even better idea postage cantilever scene

In the event you precipitate a bad scene
Do not pass goji juice to bad brain
Look through window here comes second
Sense belongs to seventh son previous
Owner said it would be okay to lie
Around with heater on, lay back, get warm

As steers go by you warm
To the task master a private scene
Wherein sundry truths do lie
You run on empty, wrack your brain
To dance through engagements previous
River deep, mountain thigh, chance second

I like to talk to you about that second Louie keeping warm
In the previous compartment you kindly let me set scene
For you and your brain on guts now knows I would not lie

GRATE

When last we are glad
Describe philosophy of money
Taken a pill to fasten
You can look it up
Everything looks regular
Bring belief relief in you yon

Hear from yon you
Only seeming seemless glad
But seamless tap tapping regular
Bell tells you *Bagman brings money*
So, if so, try looking to look very up
Use your Plato to fasten

Aristotle don't eat when fasten
Construct cave images of you yon
Broken silence brings itself up
Between courses unwrapped in Glad
Check the frequency only money
Think order the Regular

A pattern acute cuts out the regular
Ear to ground seemingly fasten
Adam Smith watches Locke the original money
Creep thru underbrush until yon you
Diogenes is very, very only too glad
The truth he never she never brings up

Hides behind the face you bring baby up
Be the regular
Makes do Demosthenes' sigh sound glad
Take a movie shoulder and fasten
Sound quality time with you yon
Currency whispers ears in serious money

It's not nothing about the money
Which ever weather market up
No, listen, the bell curve's yon you
The truth makes blink so regular
Fashion's broken heart to fasten
Relief makes the hand so-so glad

Glad amphora money reminiscence
Fasten with science look down and up
Regular words special socialize a person yon you

ORGINAL EQUIPMENT

What we were thinking of doing was to bundle
Their product with our product, shave a sliver
Off of every dime, create barriers to entry
And force the competition to break
Down to the most totally stupid
Level of not being completely lit

It's great to be stoned in comp lit
During a snowstorm, you bundle
Up and try not to look stupid
Ask *shana madle* for 'nother sliver
Given potsticker suitcase even break
Given boundless possible points of entry

It hurts like hell when you're denied entry
To a warm, aromatic and dimly lit
Chamber filled with beautiful music and break
Your leg falling down drunk, a bundle
Of nerves observing the silver sliver
Of tropic moon, but then I'm with stupid

No comment on administration because stupid
Is not my strong suit reads the last entry
In a logbook written by a boy with a sliver
In his eye in a story by H. C. Anderson. Lit-
Erature has its reasons, which comprise a bundle
Of second takes hurtling toward a line break

It's just your 19th century nervous break-
Down rubbing up against the New Stupid-
Ity in order to tell you you can make a bundle
By doing the high-school equivalent of data entry
With the sharp end of a lit
Stick burnt down to a goddamn sliver

Okay now let's slow it down just a sliver
If you keep on like that you about to break
Out in a cold sweat; before you go and do something stupid
Check it out you oughta make damn sure the pilot is lit
So you and yours can settle down raise that bundle
Of joy up in the full disclosure double daylight entry

Dark entropical gates grant entry to a sliver
Of life, a bundle of images upside an even break
What's lit up on this forehead does not spell stupid

WALK DON'T

Here make your turn
For the worse not be over
Ancients map out a plug
Modernize, don't forget your iron
Your misery becomes sand
Your song stirs the cattle

The turn made, look for cattle
Soon it's your turn
Pebbly works Ancients love to sand
When the other side's over
Laughter's rusting iron
For, today's sun is the plug

Away describes that plug
Blip tins approach cattle
Happiness e begets iron
Happiness smoothes a hot turn
Stare and stare It's over
As far as the eye can see, sand

E misery begets sand
Let's give it a plug
Bring to a boil Turn over
Thoughtfulness *encroutes* the cattle
Modern's a better way to turn
Ferocious (sic) anger melts iron

Carbon footsies steal away your iron
Ancient menus list in sand
Native patients wait their turn
Reach into pocket for a plug
Over the horizontal dip the cattle
Ancient sheepless shepherd watchover

Just when you think *Whew, over*
Yester e smotes you with iron
You now think as a cattle
Instructions run thru your mind like sand
Figuratively speaking, e finger is plug
Outlet from which Ancients turn

Turn pilaf waawaa wow over
Consultants plug e with iron
Sand steward ladle mindful cattle

WHITE VINYL SOFA

In this day the weather
The color of a taxi
We barely lie touching
See you in a while
Your way to the door
Would not treat a dog

The past can dog
You're under the weather
Your hand on the door
The jet about to taxi
We been here a while
The message is touching

The message is just touching
Base with a man about a dog
Everything goes on at once while
Nothing beats the weather
As subject-object taxi-
Dermy conversation-piece exit-door

Behind your mind there is a door
You can look but no touching
Can I call you a taxi?
Thanks. You taxi! You dog!!
How do you like this weather?
Once in a while

Multiple things happened while
You were out such as the door
Swinging open and the weather
Turning blustery, two persons touching
Each other, a woman walking a dog
And four people piling into a taxi

I used to drive a taxi
Cab until all hours while
Sensible people slept like a dog
I hitched back to my door
And wrote a diary touching
On food and drug, sex and weather

To recap, think weather, take taxi
Feel like touching sky, while
Guarding mental door, do the dog

STAND NEWS CORNER

Back on the case
Feel different it's same
Each days and every nights is battle
The Mods know, sit on the overture
Rock and whittle spit until gotta run
Bugs bang own lights only seeming

To put on their closures seeming
One leg at a time step just in case
Something insider says gotta run
The little man inside is the very same
Personality making a tiny overture
You think you hear just before battle

An old axs at the screen, a band in battle
Raiment toggles dawn's light only seeming
Early light serves its overture
As a little lawyer thinks there's maybe case
One gotta get back to one and same
Pitch forkball the sign is gotta run

Take a ride on the Reading gotta gotta gotta run
Believe you me it's a battle
Just thinking to being one and same
Language E bring to boil porridge seeming
Music in the distance is suite case
A male and female ballet brings their each overture

Um, um, each sentence overture
Into many nylon Ancients E do run
On try in vain to make a varicose case
See eye-to-eye weather total battle
Run down a fugitive kind thigh-seeming
Rooves with fabulousness if it's all the same

Outside city walls all is same
All roads lead so-and-so through overture
Arthurian paint dance steps seeming
An excitement, hold off, make you gotta run
I know, I know, it's your battle
Like or not, you know, you're some case

Case the ages they're not the same
Bring into battle your simpleton's overture
Gotta run, winks make shift seeming

THE CONFIDENCE MART

Up in the morning and off to school as Chuck Berry so
Rhythmically sings out you lay your shoulder to the big
Wheel and push that's how the day breaks no big deal
Everything is absolutely interesting when you put
A large or small amount of shelf space between yourself
Of common occasion this middle distance is the very place

Of sole proprietorship such eminent domain is no place
For this old mensch lifting that proverbial "So?"
A lot of times you find yourself
Tuned into an extra big
What-have-you when what you'd put
Up with to get out of there is a great deal

We oughta go down West Holly I hear they have a great deal
On electric wood. Do tell. I wonder what kind of place
Would sell deer antlers and light bulbs where you put
Your name in and later you get called up that's not so
Unusual I once ripped and burned an excerpt from a really big
Shoe by gum if you want something done right do it yourself

And speaking of New England why don't you go get yourself
A new mother tongue, Lou, as something you have to deal
With, along with various other requirements heretofore big
Plus being born, being borne along on back of history of place
The question mark is carried forward from *thought* to *not* so
It disappears in the oncoming rush of *call* and *put*

All of these distractions only serve to remind you to put
One foot in front of the other, one leg at a time, you yourself
Not what some person says it is like. So
What if the signals get crossed? Those are the terms of the deal
That you enter into it freely, of your own accord. A big
Reason for your being here has nothing to do with place

Everything depends on where you place
Your bets, gentlemen, and you ladies, please put
On your loveliest outfits, we're going to a big
Party, one that starts wherever you find yourself
And just as a dealer continues to deal
The cards to the last gambler, this too is not always so

The voice in the night is so out of place
It craters the deal but never mind just put
Yourself back in the picture, however much you paid to be big

NEWS BOX

Got to get me clean energy
Liquid if opposite bake
Feel meaning assemble in noise
Describe a pretty great vowel shift
Some magic empathy temporary
So, what's the big deal

So, what's the big deal
Look for your own energy
Your Dracula is (hope hope) temporary
Greet and meet, with how shake your bake
Some nights you're on the day shift
Keep inside the yellow line noise

Toe brake broken line noise
So, what's the big deal
Consonants reach over to shift
Themselves and friends have the energy
Cup after cup off to bake
Shwa more than temporary

Middle middle vowel work temporary
Reaches a finger to an ear noise
Yellow broken kisses bake
So, what's the big deal
Vigorous wash skies very energy
Put yourself in my place shift

Living making yourself is a shift
Loss of words temporary
A sounds-great combo personifies energy
At first you think *It's only noise*
So, what's the big deal
Brainstorm idea rises to bake

Deep into forest follow shaken bake
Where is the crick your feet shift
So, what's the big deal
This construction zone is temporary
Walk around with all this noise
Being an undead has its own energy

Believe any energy can bake
Noise they make the feet shift
Temporary, so what's the big deal

AUTUMN LEAVES GOES

3/22/12

THE TREES, being dumb, as people go, green, leave a
month early.

> Later, blah blah blah
> (Kick the cat)
> Where's that shit

there is a general feeling in the land, deserve the name
of white something something (those who imagine same)
interest in race and money, abroad in the land *I'm being
followed.*

> Come from where
> (Do the dog)
> Et cetera et cetera

medical adventures in election, increments mend. going out.
getting used to the thanks. thoughts on the battle Kurz finish-
ing the heart in Eichmann in Jerusalem via Hilberg.

> Night
> Night
> Night

today I'm rooting around and I come across your letter of
12/19. a familiar cat got your tongue takes pen to paper (yoga)
from which exit my not-very-true words, how can they be very.

american english, let that be our back roads, and dig around for scenic routes and overlooks and beautiful turnouts. the balance sheen shall blind us re Merce.

> Clothes flap
> Three deep
> Fill *gris gris*

his classical eminence. done ermine.

3/27/12

CLEAR THE decks, walking-around money, on-street visor,
sufficient unto the day, as it is only ever this.

> Turn
> See nothing
> That special nothing

drop down mineshaft, working in a coal, nothing can stop,
Manny on bongos ditto. what on end are mountains, rivers,
earth, human beings, animals, and houses?

> Seeing past being
> Into an intersection
> Men working

young folks building companies, works, outta every fact ever
coined, mint julep, Kentucky ham, now at our fingertips,
clickety-clack, fat talk track. meanwhile, and there usually is
one, how you get from, here meets there, is up to you.

it would be an honest day's wonk, to be sore. friends and
neighbors catch up at the meet-up.

> Great sweater
> Really love the shoes
> And the watch!

See you later
You're the best
Don't peek!

your note to self is a rigorous trumpet of style. I'm still trying
to peel myself off the floor/ceiling. the whole she-bang is one

bright pool, as necessary as it is one. carry your country across
itself, says who, a while back-to-back, a string o' lazy Sundays.

ONCE AGAIN, alone with her thoughts, is that special someone. many a year ago in the past lives of the poets.

> Looking for nature's address
> The lives of the poets are wives
> A sex shakes hands with

frequently words to songs run like bunny slippers through the genome brain. Take it up with Plato annoying again. "Ari, let us reason in the season. A cuff slippery opry plectrum. Naughts make way, you fools, for the blogs. Fasten your hardwares."

> Mighty beat yearning
> Enter rooms on tippy toes
> Buddha is one down

too fucken much. place back of hand (either/both) upon brow.

> Guests of rain
> Word soups
> Sop thesaurus

you pull up to yon beggar and beg forgiveness, the revival is a giant snake handle car door.

absolutely no needles doth they give themselves, for they are masons, part of the innie. None of their old friends stop by. recent photo. and only one snifter. over a candle roll bulbish glass over votive candle and cast your vote in the serf working hard to pay back student loans to heir eventual masters.

> Great sweater
> Really love the shoes
> And the watch!

freshets. some grommets. gusts.

BUCKETS OF rain, juggle bread, ink, car keys, inverse
umbrella, into and out of, versions of the neighborhood.
Come in and dry off.

> On the corner
> What's left out
> Make space for

Used story, out of it. Sleep is nothing. Car to train, then bus,
stops driven bat shit, night same again but backwards, on
fumes. Mind the gap. Rudolph Cupertino. Why do? Inch sync,
flat vistas, slash skies, portable foot, breathe your list, hip
lectern, crossing Milpitas.

> *Excusez-moi* tendons
> Left outside ears
> Wonder what else

Scratch at vague word moss, places poetry used to go. Messed
up trails cascaded a while back, can't see diddly, but now wow
thousand-year pop-up, ache waivers, an eyeful tower of old.

> An olden days move
> Flick the flea
> World looks like everywhere

Everywhere behind Doug fir *sayonara*, brings home fact
cheek-to-cheek is (not) forever, get in sadness pool, at
Matanzas a bell buoy loop. That day a non-seeing eye plays
Bruca Manigua and/or sings *Foggy Mountain Breakdown*.
Not like your Black-Eyed Keys, trad in the boonies and good
on them.

> Minstrelsy in relief
> Accordion to you
> Voice magnificent

My dream a date with Aretha Franklin. Big data moves
mountains, celebrity elevator buttons blink, algorithms offer
up aggregate typica, dynamic operations coalesce in air. Leap
clear of the moving platform.

Having a topped ball
Crazy great curvature
Refrain passengers will please

REMEMBER THE day your doctor told you you can have an erection. calm down, Plato, calm down. that's better, you can do this.

Tremendous logic
Creams phenomenology
Diva philatelically correct

the repression OF, incline to go to, a little more blue. whole other life, border on borrow use, recognize *les fleurs.* Aristotle even calls it marvelous, for unknown to him the americans already speak american english as says the man in the streets, name of James, answers to Jim, hey, Jim, come into the little town on the quiet waters, where are the slippers (them again) the wind wears as breeze.

Throw displaced person
Campfires inner distance
The batter and a layer

and then, nothing happens, sorta novellas. we lose a boatload of those jobs a month ago the overall pool of numbers going down, for trail follow blazes, a person we turn to. doing it too fast too cheap. fog covers grease (not the country, altho similar similitude) a longing bird calls alma alma. be careful, you're showing too much acknowledge info succulent like a beatnikette thigh foraged in the lounge. the trail gets steeper. factor in as a time trial in which the jury is out.

Invariable feet
Two twisters touch down
Plow thru godzilla truck

look for a good job job. like the women who are real and the men who realize. the inner Plato hating the poets, what a macaroon, *is that so.*

Slip in a mountain
Couple of villages
Tiny quote people

Quail dove
And stone on tv
There's whosis

PASSING THROUGH fields of garbage, the syntactical
hero pulls the trigger on meant verbiage, shoots the object
of his rampant longitude, dead predicate, and rides off into
the archaic, trailing diaphanous interpellations. How the
West Was. one should always think and say that being is,
Parmenides thinks out loud, but Heraclitus already left.

> Let's do some philosophy
> Health is coercive supremes say
> Let's gamify this sucka

sun up in rafters. get on El, ride to Loop. distance of board
feet. heard a million times but Soldiers Field in the rain's
magnifique, comparable to *Up Periscope*.

> Checking my figuratively watch
> I got bupkis
> Trails leading back to interior

competitive takedowns are physical, energetic pressure points
that help companies be awesomer.

> We sing boisterously to our pillows
> Every citizen's a right-to-bear device
> Flood the gaps

human mic check, testing one two. written altogether, then assigned to so-called authors for credit at the general store. they don't talk like that where I come from. malware, phishing and botnets never touch your skin. america is complexity, not nation, empire, difference built in. until entropic white exchange value collar buttons down for the talented tenth. beautiful *guerillas* with large dogs lope through forest.

> History goes
> Extra mile
> Wrap head around

there was not so much as a sound. then cicadas.

> Alone with her thoughts
> Maple leaves
> Stick to the ground

UP IN the morning and out to school. swan ampersands the
butter knife of science heat therapy reveals: ah, body (beat)
mind (beat) refresh (no beat).

> White house front doorway
> Change into worn writing
> Handpick each sleeve

oh, sure. despite what *you* think. today's another day.
mysterious stranger clint eastwood comes to town with
hemlock air freshener for the whole town to take. and they do.

so plausibly denial, say it ain't so, scare the hell out of the
country. (my turn) ruling nest of vipers chop shop the
elections encrypted by the primaries, only way far. you're not
your own person.

> Snow upon the hood
> Sway, birches, sway
> To and Bob froth

nature's addressee, really loves that Socrates, and the
WATCHIT. thought progress meat, ola Salome, way, down
dumb as shit. secrets outta sight, only believe, your lying
eyes. hair interrupts perfect, stands on the end of the line,
the bobber niblets.

A chuckling big softee
Shrug shoulders bounce
Utterance come forward

a body of special knowledge with its special source resplen-
dent, and fluent, in hamburger.

an american variable zut alors.

BANANA REPUBLICANS usher usa into twenty-first-century
third world. honey I shrunk the people. gentlemen prefer
secret services while 82nd airborne poses with parts. it's how
we roll.

> Take a powder
> Put it in the books
> You're late

page at a time. blurred lines. what it takes to not even notice.
duly recording in a sow's ear. musicking in common, do
not die, do not pass thru, do not collect $200. an hour is an
approximate increment.

> Early to bed
> Early to rise
> Early admissions

anything calm is strange. hat on a bed, hamster wheel
thoughts, like there's no tomorrow. meanwhile, and there
usually is, others are occupied, playing, swimming, lazy. talk
to you later.

> Up late
> Up in arms
> Up yours

don't mind commute. sun up in siren time, train horn dinette.

optimization is essential – random guesses – hard numbers –
don't wanna brag about integration – to a broken system.

learn how to play without rules – InstaGrok – it only takes one
big one. where's the sauce? cold in the shade. rail lines,
commercial real estate, spam filters, hoodies, pot smoke,
traffic. statements of work unfold as phase-of-moon progress.

SO HOW'S by you. you think. for crime out loud just check
each others' notebooks. what's not to like. we ilk. the cat
calls it a day. anita. oh. where one thing leads to another,
no question. et tu Socrate.

> Luminol rights
> Take constitutional
> Die on the die job

funny guy laff. that's with two f's. no ugh. because I love you,
the table, because I love you. head in hands, where's the rest,
a nice fan. music fold turn a corner corridors.

> Safe
> On a bathrobe
> To first

win lose or draw, the line moves, all any everybodies. this is
false in any prom. how you hold your head. timely than ever
corsage.

you're a big man, a big man.

> Frog hops
> One thought
> One think

require apostrophe, write in for, weather jumpity. shiny big motes. cat's bon mots. some ghostly nouns. this is you, this is me, then this. smile falls, apart, meant to mean. an all nylon breakfast. air under wings. nice work you get.

down thru the ages, that crazy cuckoo, 800 number. a big hole, give a holler, glimpse what's. steps of chubway, onto platform, tile wall down.

> Yeah, this works
> Getting lite out
> It's a fine line

4/26

WHEN IN doubt, top of head off. instant opposite, the minus
train time loop of day. your converse sensation picks up where
a rest takes up time, a crack in. munch to report as storm
clouds brew coffee in Antietam.

> Civil war general
> Gets lost in swamp
> Later writes *Ben Hur*

insurance workarounds undermine water rights in luxury
hotels. here's a big long list of names, spell something. we're
not running for conga line here, sweet peas climbing the
sides, get back in your chair and crank. outta band, outta line.

> One man's nerves
> Freak the house
> Sit outside a while

who we are at work is different. bragging and asking for
advice are naturally social, it's ok, flirt with crocodile, carve
niche behind firewall. back into the forest of nerds. shelf life
of info is quick. structure implies permanence, sure, but
chronology is not relevance, we can agree on that.

> Stuck in Soviet Union
> Too tall, can't hear
> What's the big deal?

who we are is work differently. tall grass of *waa*. turn down big sky dimmer at eod. a cloud service is rain. birds, not angry, tweet best who tweet first, a light breeze that stays. is that something heavy rolling on pavement or someone beating sticks on plastic tubs? define neighborhood. waking to work. dreams to die for.

> Last light
> Reflects on rain surface
> Concentric drops dissolve

4/27

HOW'S BY you? read spicier number, watch yanks at
play, bawling over a plate. window across the way, backlit
giant screen (how you spell screen). stop before the start.
powderish bluish, in the next issue. smooth a green address,
remember said street, toothpick tonguetip.

> Psychology's sleeping bag
> Crawl in a crying jag
> Groundcloth's animal cries

thinking murky chrome, words in the buff, preview later
summer.

> Clear eye
> And throat
> And out

wires dance, wind noise, poems made (totally jack up).

> Dottie Dottie
> I hear your train
> Aw, come on

> Breviary greens
> Puffy whites
> Zat blues

underwears and something. know better, said the room,
pancake data, no big deal, boat against tide, right up.

take human insects, life threatening conditions, you, less pain.
sun decides today go on, tomorrow gone.

don't think I'll forget, thumbnail, do with, how, I'll tell you.

> Breathe acrostic
> Any comments
> Select moonphase

street missing, fourth story and up, true blue. is the *might*
change the gear, ok, pass tense. too tired to brag. that was
close. is.

PAINT SELF out of corner. ask about heart v. ice. send me
your ours. try one of moon (yellow highlights).

> Use it or lose it
> R u ready to yammer?
> My worthy retainer

by any means necessary, mutual sat, jack-of-all-trads. then
drive over to the bakery for the gig. I honked, but you were
engaged in convolution. right near here.

> Taco truck
> Light rain
> Lotta nice friends

the suit is a hoot. when no work, relax. simplicity, speed and
scale. the momentum mantra. big close moon be full tonight.
all my ancient twisted car parts born of green hail and
diffusion I do now secretarially avow. wampum for gummies.

> No matter how
> Think you know
> Spring rains

time unwinds. them bell full, light metal jack, pick up stills.
he's a nice man. I love him.

EVERYTHING DIFFERING, pull yourself together, man
(slapslap). needs that. those days, look olden, they me.

> Great stuff in between
> You treat me so bad
> Cry into loving shoulder

point and shucks, fingers, count off, the big draw.

> Walk up
> Look great
> Dumb down

stuff in the park, hear it's beautiful, is bleeving C. stand
outside, along the way, sort of thing. we want to get this
appraised, see what the guy thinks. very fragile. some bible
slut, with the fallen, you know, and they go out. ask me *which
hand,* it's worth under underline, subtitles.

> Or as they say
> What the hey
> No way

head tip level off. person is isn't crazy, make up mind bed. a
go-to move, the new-looking way, sort of wings swoop.

Dot dish green
Birds hop twigs
Bar gone chittery cheapie

something off, head barely on neck, regardless weather. fresh
white blossoms, money for meds, where, red brick cream
lintels. top 5, no doubt, a quart and screen place, a tearing of
silk. smell yourself, like no other, lox sunset.

About here
Windy twig shadows
Put them up

TENSION BETWEEN people and topics. don't tread on my hover card. people's brands? I thought people were just people. don't be silly. don't be left out. so afraid of missing something they love the company.

> Consumers gather
> In virtual *zocalo*
> Now never not at work

faster pussycat kill kill. spin up a service pronto. first mover advantage. time to think later. ask questions later. worry later. dare to be bold. hammer down on the crush points. jack-be-nimble track shoes name that pizza. everybody has their own sound track.

> Our methodology
> Our architecture
> Our interface

my word. up at all hours in a blizzard of notes. no time to capitalize after each period. accounting is discipline, a way to exhaust possibility, fall out of body, check out of mind, drive the blue truck tipped over on its side, slide sideways over the slippery surface of the interstate from behind the cab. touch brakes lightly when I say so. c u later. have a good one.

The train passes
Under the bay
Through an echo chamber

falling into her device. see what's said. buy card. track usage
online. which one is me? whose feet in whose shoes?
up in the morning and off to skill sets, on-boarding exercise
at least as good as. summer opera law school dining room
to combat eye fatigue. she looks ok at herself. then braids a
strand of information alongside her face.

Underground levels
Open into
Vast flights of migratory birds

surrealism is out of service at this time. go a different way.
do not swivel head around backwards. stand on marble floor
in a moment from now. often seen inching into abeyance.
otherwise certain to arrive safely before long.

Remember who said what
Bow-and-arrow suspension bridge
On way to ballpark

different tunes on ear buds. aqua sugar nipple, aqua shades.
put some hair stuff on. lip sync along. hot pink nail polish.
look out window, check device. yep, lipstick. end of day, end of
week, emptying out of commerce.

Day a round trip
Shock of random eye contact
Views of roofs

ASTOUND FRIENDS survive the smell test, leaf smoke, as I
wondered like a crowd.

> Middle of nowhere
> How's that
> The peony

no double bag needs, the elastic rose of summer, watch your
hands, them. fill with non-state actors. the irony curtain rises
on the wait-a-second act. listen to yourself, talk up a storm,
today's sky. only in so far as, puff puff, deep almost blue. the
rain spoke Ann, it's a wash, clear, let's not go there, it

> The season finale
> I want answers
> A two bath day

don't ask them for directions.

> The side of caution
> Protocol follow
> The assume not done

losing light, siren past tense, green, tweets. it's the country's
foot, door slide eyes open, a little bit morning Bach, look in
the ointment.

Tip sombrero
Over eyes
Long short shadows

rainy miffed, siren doubles, for your love. wind in shadows,
hand-writing edges, make out words. understand the hair,
your dreams come truer, it is there that magic. worry.
nothing. about. driving the vote, crazy about you baby, wailing
choochoo. show acne who's Boss, they call me Mr. Lucky,
different edges calendar.

Batchy fog
Partial clearing
Late 60s

Note flow, a flower, no relation. hands out, IDIOTS, do a
funny wave, one of many Joes. notice how, you don't notice,
them then do.

MAN AT hut says "from here to the 60s, with a high mention
to cross out and the paper trail mare's nest in tatters, better get
a guy or gal to take you over." so we hire a young killer joe type,
blade ready, joystick at ease, & off we go. feels like just the day
to sort on edge, then the inward shiver. like man say, the city is
high, dense, above bird, in deep air like groping for pillow. feels
like dirt from fat clouds, push push on through shiny bamboo,
wade H2O, stub rock, cold sweat, finally come out in Miami.
our guy says "wow we made it, no adventures." we're like wow.

at Obamazawa visit dude name Seethru. loaded but not lame.
from trips to Mumbai he digs road fry, has us chill many days
after being so much on the go, cools us all kinda way.

> Nice
> Self to home
> Kickin' it

> Lay down
> Six eight under four
> Old style

as fish, no end to water. as bird, no end to air. we are "in it."

> From boat sea looks round
> Isn't
> Is actually more like jungle gym

while writing you "writing you" got drenched in car wash,
passenger window open. stupid humid. the period's a
conversation stopper, the comma leads on, piling a pair o'
taxies onto the curb, when who should emerge from revolving
door but It Girl, her lapdog Bitty in tow. you had a be there.

   Alone with her thoughts
   Pine needles
   Stick to point

climb along edges, creep over popovers, ship out from head,
deepen scene, live air, open letter.

   Nada sound
   Stone still
   Cicada only

NO NO no, the finger shakes in the face, if and when. many
aficionados regard it's a wonder avocados. getting by trying
avoid the extra things in life you tell me who's this Plato guy.

> The point detail
> Breeze thru screen
> Smells real go

> If not a moment
> (Too soon) a moment
> Be there in (therein)

are they any good, real good, it can't be bad. don't get
carried away, belong to the village, tease out freak
infrastructure. summer's if here, winterize the car away,
ride out each sound, walk through mammal, a torn sheep,
pen a bend note. dan's man tan snow, young birches slight
sway, picking up after itself, spitting farm days, just ridiculous
crap, clouds floridian.

> Barebones moon
> Supply rent tears
> Drop off at corner

why's the (forget), leave off word extras, soliliquy spelled
wrong air. whoever's whim, adjust slightly, botanical phrase.

Trouble sleeping
Look for trouble
My shwa

weather missing, it's unheard of, on a tray, the catheter of,
thee new reality show, twitch delay, give a for instance, the
honest sound, tells truthie. yellowy looking light, the face
lights up, come down a peg, in an endgame, back to back,
come on down, match day, on the installment plan, men with
flaming hair.

Collapsible inwardness
Ghost winters on the sly
Dark and windy day or so

Brisk glass
Clean feet club
Ditto so prove

Loud sparrow
Windblown new leaves
Not even summer

LOOKS LIKE nada, unless rainy delay. then coach can get
up in your grill. you brought your axe? put it here. we have
mobile irons in the fire. there is more philosophy from
continents other than Europe than in all of your dialectics.

hi-def cave wall. whatever you think it's more than.

> *La rumba*
> *N'est-ce pas salé*
> Signals from Africa

urban dance is not salty. *gandinga, mondongo, sandunga.*
before Plato made banana split. before even Pluto was planet.

prose hits wall when grass grows greener on other side bet.

> Here ago minute
> Now does not
> Wind flam

go in car round rocky cliffs in full sun with music on and visit
friend about to move to other coast after many years help save
files. everything can be said in threes, birth, death, you-name-
it. save the best for first.

I could talk to you for flowers.

CEO turns 40
Exit strategy
Let them eat cake

ceo turns forty, sells company, throws Louis XVI bash at
LA villa, hires Snoop Dogg, gets back to work, still grumpy.
where's the cake?

Pacific fog
Blows fast
Overhead

the work of crowded cubes opens out into worlds of consumer
choice. occupy air. drink wash swim. feet on ground. burn
nervous.

Chatter traffic
Bird bent on next sec
Just show up

7/19

CUT TO the blurb read, don't believe, you're sick, honey does
your makeup, don't that, don't, keep your hands. the new
moon, quotes science, for its since.

> Breeze blows
> Thru mind
> Inside mine

> The everyday
> Recedes into sunset
> Long time coming

tip sombrero, over eyes, long short shadows, it's coming back,
feel free to leave, a fresh tree.

> Head ache
> Night's pill
> Insiders

things change, people change, couldn't have things. wise
beyond years, nerves of steel, comes with job. as dogs, *in a
minute*, be there-er. really, the weather's so nice, take a look-
see.

> Screen
> Breeze
> Meow

fucken A-right, game-call weather, no outs. too rhyme, win-
dow left, fable air. we rose quarterly, alive with nickels, each
dollar too sad. compare to what, (owl), light pup. a victim of
foul play, the guy next door, the day after all. check today's
greens, sunny blues, no pun tend pan.

Pronoun to mirror
Alas, me too
Molasses, moi aussi

sun, walking out into, not so easy does it, nor moving on,
not so.

Blue brass dish dish
Walk the floor
The chronic shoes

Closing the door
Trying not to here
Revealing of the glint

whimsy passes thru the screens, not a cloud for up around
miles, soprano miles to each up degree. enter the language,
the side door, screen bangs, talking away, more at home,
come up, body closing in, bird discography, mood morpheme,
behind the wheel, the driving range, a drawing board.

There
Looking up
You're there, right

Smoke hangs up
On the mist
Maybe later

whippoorwill closes, for the day, thanks, call again.

MUSIC ROUNDS corner, out-of-door, off-to-work streets, in-
and-out time, a saunter, a blast of port air, salty, sumptuous,
manage as best you able. decisive manifold articulation, all
the way up and down the line.

>Farmers market parking
>Laundromat locker room store
>Walk on by

>Line of swimmers
>Stretch out marker to marker
>Straight as that

there is in every day the baffling principle of whatsis, pushing
the living daylights out of the arranged marriage (heaven
and hell), singular, bent on repetition, falling away from
remittance.

>Motor next door
>Take what you can get
>In the air

>No one can say
>Excellent silence
>Late sun red plum

so witchly reworded, toxy environs rain down crazy money on
dysfunctionary katzenjammers. fuck you money. new recruits
vs. eight-legged freaks in cyberspace. it's all in good from.

many stages develop layered thick in mountain earth, hats off
to former times. remember with sigh, seal with kiss, as tears
go by.

> Slow blossoms
> Remarkable stubbornness
> Double-digit snow

open the door. trees arm the image. embrace ambien sound.
you could say that.

TOUCH BASES full of *ehs* it's all about a chopper shot, an apartment, shooter. 6 months, as the third person, you know, a lone woof, listen to travel record, copycat. smooth a green address, toothpick tongue tip, need a lot of *thoses* to get there, light only if *with*.

>The part
>You don't get it
>Where you get it

ever be true, mine 4ever, babybaby.

>Rainy day
>Acrostic wave
>Rumor view

okay, I'm at the subway, see you, ten minutes. no, no, grassy explain, insidious rainy.

>Rain jewelry
>Clearing
>And me too

the little old man, act, no act, when think back on. salute, just in general, frontsie. pictures to go to, bleeding marquee, now playing turquoise.

A moment of clam
Crabby pinky horseshoe ring
Someonette door

Not quite there
Face, look out
Eyes real flat

a committee 4ever, a cami loup, wind tweeze browbeat. O
prednisone, Aristophanes spooks thus, remedial gossamer
mosts. there comes a time, watch where you're walking, an
eye's sharp stick.

Looks like
Shadows
Say so if you

Money put to music
Play *babybaby*
Rounding daily error

STARS FELL on Al Obama. PO has money after all. parks
hiding money. cardboard all caps: FUCK YOU PAY ME. it's
nice outside.

> Feeling welling up
> A timely pass
> On the money

> Goes without say-so
> Feeling left in
> Out to get you

is this a booty call? wound up tighter than a drummer. both
sides of mouth. when bad thing happens, stop, reflect light,
pack heat, two by two by. it's a malled world.

> Don't be that way
> Approximate timeframe
> Jagged edges

says something about. more waves where came from. four
wait cycles max. you kidding me? outta there. into intersec-
tional traffic, sluice gate *communitas* on-ramp to bridge big
water. hand out window, down, air sideways, rubber to road.

Wind cries Manny
Back next week
Thanks for asking

an empty space of air in which to air what-have-I out.
interesting emblematics. word battles. juice states.

Four bar break
At end of Night
In Tunisia

ROLL DOWN the windows, relax, it's what it's all about (there
for you). I don't know what's it to me but it is to me. a village
volleyball, clinging to its mist, net net.

a pump gas twilight, actual pampas grass, clear blue on
trestle initials beautiful color, in dew on the hood, with heart
thru arrow.

> Warm air
> Meets cool water
> Word to the wise

black spot, formerly known as gum, chew the fat.

> Deep in heart
> Another heart
> Fill til glass

> Come in
> Comes in
> Read paper

> Parking apiece
> Guessing brush skin
> Fold slow

the short sentence, how are them, too, try on in a native
language, leave half off, quit worry about, windy greens. couch
arm, leaving on, where am. body takeaway, me never no never,
the mention soap. eyeballs on the street, subject leave building,
felony predicate in play. doll eye cue ball, arrange Iraq, get the
rest freefall.

> Wrong feel
> Wrong weight
> Ink sinks in

> Tongue pokes around
> Snowy, hilly
> A fir cloud

oh, hell, a busybody don't be. but like, say, plan foregone exit,
count as vowel. skittery words shit, what's this all. . .ah, it's
sunday. reading, look up, it's, oh, it's (glance). eye turns, into
ear, anguish in vowels' comma, shoulder, semicolon craze.
this way to exception, fine kettle (u's wish). start ingenuity,
nicely breezes.

> A picture
> Today's pick
> Some day's weather

> Copy the cat
> The dog one
> A horse's mouth

sorta out of sorts, all sorts is candy, bells and dog whistles.

> Breadcrumb moonlight
> And there's the following
> Trees and stones dance dozens

8/6

BUSY DUSTING off your XYZ. placeholder meeting of king
salamander brothers' mines. don't wanna be late. hate to be
early. glad when over. lit out for territory, never to be scene
again.

Play for peanuts
Salted in shell
Meta world peep

soup-to-*bada-boom asana*. car locked, motor running. all in a
day, the works.

don't want the pressure, stay home and cook. hand-to-hand
beauty marks time. each is in his or her bird or fish life,
every which way. otherwise, not. and even then. seeming in
summer.

That was then
This is now
Pasta fazool

Splattered with mud
Wet with water
Only a matter of time

bits and pieces is how we do our day. you go out and meet
someone. someone meets someone. you meet yourself. going
out meets going out.

> Wind in leaves
> Leaves in wind
> Which is it?

chilly morning attitude perfunction. enough to lift a line
of trees. experimental finger work. concept masking in the
upper branches, a long note followed by an abrupt fracking
sound. up 'n' at 'em.

> Study philosophy carefully
> Sit on militant mile
> Container frappe

> Big plum sky
> Dizzy from aether
> Think too much

somewhat your somewhat elevator shoes mention in stain
class buoyancy waivers, look booth ways, step off curb, beware
at an angle. you add absolutely to free you get splash.

> Just add weather
> A winning smile
> Surface of Mars

THAT BEING SAID

Catch an eye
On the road again
Brush fingers' legend

COGNITIVE BEHAVIORAL THEREMIN

Outside your ken
World keeps going
Our arms end in all hands on deck

Anonymize weather
Homemade say no evil
Unlocket trunk line

Pray to Virgin
Rid of Putin
Pussy Riot

[YOU] CAN BE

The word Bosses
Their limbs enplane
Secrets liken tweeners

OCHOCINCO MI AMOR

Jim Dandy
Bo Diddly
Puff Diddy

Oh, shit, totally
The head falls
Moon upon its bell

Leveling process
Action of animals
Wheel ruts over time

Dew knocked off
Okay, tracks mean animals
No wildlife, no hi, cue

Chill user, no hassles
Armed at idle
Does not ruin your life

Playa pays tutu
So fond yellow tape
Asleep in past pup

Turnkey diner
Ex-planet folderol
Incidental fa-so-la

Without a prayer
Backlit cloudy
Slight limbo radio

Big ordinary signs
Heavy men in situ
The golden what

Hour combs nearer
Tortoise shell clouds
Up in the hair day

In-flight revolutionary feeling
Facts out the window
Life in the wild

The unknown begins
Here goes nuthin
The color *rock*

Saturday night flubber
What's it to ya
Jam jar all along

MOVING CRIME SCENE

Breeze shake infancy fists
Dawn self-cheerlead
Enter *win a trip to*

Local hero
Walt Whitman
American soil

Off the shoulder
Hanging on
Little (hmm) smile

Small of back
Ten large
Why wouldn't you

Don't kiss ass
(How beautiful)
To be broke

Back pocket bounce
Dot i's cross t's
Other lights up

Screw shape sunset
Serenity's an illusion
Delusion rain

Same day surface
Emotional intel
Reading something blue

Dawn my shadow
Shade pulls up
Blue jay into blue

Sleep thru paper
Rice milk man
No breeze at all

Tonic in the gun
Dial late limes mileage
Pretty damn near lost it

Put lime in coconut
Get out kitchen and dance
Sparkling fallback day

Torso find in lake
Get here how'd I
Spring comes up shorts

Mexico return bottle to
Chair comfy hurt on
Charlie horse

FATTY CRUST NOTES

Head rub info
Nice nice
Read paper day

FOXY BROWN FOX

Ice maker cometh
Coffee and a taco
The same

A HOT EXTRACT

Tear eyeward
Strangers wordified
Chilly teeth slippers

Squeeze-on U
Fox con phone smarts
Throw student body

Fall four hour hardon
If you think *have to*
Bring to a boil serve

ARKADIIANA

Stop dead in trucks
At once in head
Parade me no rain

LAWYER UP

Nyuk nyuk
Scissory *hey whoa*
Lo & yo

THICK BUSH

Own beeswax
Hod on head
Draw a bead on *on*

Styrofoam weather
Nibbling sparrow
Sunny leaf

UMBRELLA

At work
On the go
Everywhere

Asunder road
Close suppose
Nitwits' *thises*

Water hotter
Noise next doors
Silent leaves

SECURE THE PERIMETER

Fall day falls
Accent gravity
Game-used dirt

Easy does what
Slip on slide rule
Talk to the table

IF SAY SO

Islands of excellence
Palms out
Singing in wood

BLUB MED

Give it up shoulders
Square chest silvery treasure
Buried in backyard might

TAKE 2

Sans iambic pants
Like it's nobody's business
Windowy glash flashes

INBOX OUTTAKE

Hopped up on sports shirts
Two-day beard when you have time
Parental contrails

Soy tweed quibbles
Tears of merrimento
Stream 80% goody feel

Yo soy un hombre silencio
Horizon at sea 360
Fish palace sky gem space

YOUR GENTLE BODY

Lines crisscross south of the bit
But this is a waltz
The ankle directs my attention
This, too, is altitude

Then over in the second
Something or other, this is must lateness
I'm intentionally delay
Within several momentum's carbons

The covers parts lumens
Swing against the laughter the joules
Carry smoke away from the table
But frittering away each opportunity
The travel of which you're surely aware

Thinking *this* is tardiness
I tune in this station

The people are many

Who are winterized

The fourth sound entering their throats
Began with froths
And a great stamping boot
Finishing each dance

Then each dancer turned to their corner
Where the answer to the mystery to the mystery

Became something how you say it
With the returning boom of the whosis
And in anterior rooms
This burns with houses
And houses great birds

In an open wing

Flaunted with geraniums
The time is now

And then

ROOF BOOKS

the best in language since 1976

Recent & Selected Titles

- **Vile Lilt** by Nada Gordon. 114 p. $14.95
- **Dear All** by Michael Gottlieb. 94 p. $14.95
- **Flowering Mall** by Brandon Brown. 112 p. $14.95.
- **ONE** by Blake Butler & Vanessa Place.
Assembled by Christopher Higgs. 152 p. $16.95
- **Motes** by Craig Dworkin. 88 p. $14.95
- **Apocalypso** by Evelyn Reilly. 112 p. $14.95
- **Both Poems** by Anne Tardos. 112 p. $14.95
- **Against Professional Secrets** by César Vallejo.
Translated by Joseph Mulligan.
(complete Spanish/English) 104 p. $14.95.
- **Split the Stick: A Minimalist-Divan**
by Mac Wellman. 96 p. $14.95

Roof Books are published by
Segue Foundation
300 Bowery • New York, NY 10012
Visit our website at seguefoundation.com

Roof Books are distributed by
SMALL PRESS DISTRIBUTION
1341 Seventh Street • Berkeley, CA. 94710-1403.
Phone orders: 800-869-7553
spdbooks.org